Exploring the Rain Forest

Mattias Klum & Hans Odoo

Sterling Publishing Co., Inc.
New York

Translation edited by Jeanette Green
Translated from the Swedish by Mirja Tornquist

Scientific Consultant—Dr. Nancy B. Simmons, Assistant Curator,
American Museum of Natural History, Department of Mammalogy

Library of Congress Cataloging-in-Publication Data

Klum, Mattias.
    [På upptäcktsfärd i regnskogen. English]
    Exploring the rain forest / Mattias Klum and Hans Odoo.
      p.   cm.
    Includes index.
    Summary: Describes the variety, beauty, and interrelatedness of
plant and animal life found in rain forests in Costa Rica, Brazil,
Nigeria, and Borneo.
    ISBN: 0-8069-9873-3
    1. Rain forests—Juvenile literature.   2. Rain forest ecology—
Juvenile literature. [1. Rain forests.   2. Rain forest ecology.
3. Ecology.]   I. Odoo, Hans. II. Title.
QH86.K5813   1997
578.734—dc21   97-19631

1   3   5   7   9   10   8   6   4   2

Published 1997 by Sterling Publishing Company, Inc.
387 Park Avenue South, New York, N.Y. 10016
Originally published by Rabén & Sjögren, Stockholm, Sweden
under the title *På upptäcktsfärd i regnskogen*
© 1995 by Mattias Klum (photography) and Hans Odoo (text)
English translation © 1997 by Sterling Publishing Co., Inc.
Distributed in Canada by Sterling Publishing
% Canadian Manda Group, One Atlantic Avenue, Suite 105
Toronto, Ontario, Canada M6K 3E7
Distributed in Great Britain and Europe and Cassell PLC
Wellington House, 125 Strand, London WC2R 0BB, England
Distributed in Australia by Capricorn Link (Australia) Pty Ltd.
P.O. Box 6651, Baulkham Hills, Business Centre, NSW 2153, Australia
Printed in Hong Kong

Sterling ISBN 0-8069-9873-3

Inside cover: *Rain forest in Malaysia.*

Contents

Mattias Klum, photographer, and Hans Odöö, author.   Photo by Monika Klum

Welcome to the Rain Forest!

It's morning. Our camp is by a river, and we just went for a swim in the tepid water. My name is Hans and I'm the author. Mattias, with the camera on his lap, is the photographer.

We think the rain forest is fantastic! There are so many amazing and beautiful things to explore here. We really cherish that. But we're not only here to savor it. We also want to show and tell everyone about the rain forest—so that more people will want to help save it. Perhaps even you.

Come with us in this book to visit rain forests around the world.

Greetings from *Mattias* and *Hans*

Mossy tree roots in the rain forest.

Inside the Fantastic Rain Forest

Most tropical rain forests are located in countries and on islands along the equator. Although rain forests cover only 7 percent of the earth's surface, inside them are more plant and animal species than in all the rest of the world.

Here, in the rain forest, you can encounter the most peculiar creatures. And the most beautiful!

But many rain forest plants and animals don't want to be seen. So, sometimes you can walk and walk and walk, and look and look and look, without seeing anything but green, green, green.

Over 170,000 plant species are in the world's rain forests. This orchid is just one of them. Malaysia

Poison dart frogs are tiny. There are many different species; most have bright colors. Here are two males wrestling. Costa Rica

But soon, from within all the green, a lovely flower reveals itself. Or, all of a sudden, a green leaf walks away on six small insect legs. Two bright red frogs, no larger than raspberries, roll around on the ground in a wrestling match between Lilliputians.

Then all is once again green and still.

You can easily tell from the name that it rains a lot in the rain forest. It actually rains at least ten times more in the rain forest than in other parts of the world where tall trees also flourish, like the British Isles and northern Europe, southeastern Canada and the northeastern United States. Rain forests get between 70 and 200 inches (180 to 500 centimeters) of rain a year. The temperature in the rain forest is from 70 to 80° Fahrenheit (21 to 27° Centigrade) or higher, day and night, year-round.

Insect camouflaged as a leaf. Nigeria

Macaws. Brazil

Atlas moth. Malaysia

All of a sudden the sky is full of color!

The world's largest parrots, macaws, fly above our heads. They are a combination of red, blue, yellow, and white. One bird in this company of parrots cocks its head in curiosity and looks at us. Just as quickly as they appeared, they disappear. Once again, all is green and still.

Such is the rain forest. One moment all you can hear is the constant chirp of katydids, and all you can see are all these perpetually green plants. Then, for a few fleeting moments a camouflaged butterfly opens its wings and displays its rich colors . . .

High up in a tree, a monkey becomes angry with his friend and pinches him so that he cries out loudly.

Then everything again becomes green and still.

The black spider monkey prefers to hang out high in the trees. Its prehensile tail acts as a fifth hand. Brazil

River in Brazil.

Up the River

The sun has not yet risen. We hear rattling sounds from down by the beach. It's our guides, natives of the rain forest, attaching the motor to the boat. We are still catching our breath after unloading our gear from the jeep. Morning can be cool in the rain forest, but now we are sweating profusely.

We have several hours' journey ahead of us. We are approaching a region untouched by humans. The natives take the opportunity to search for larvae to use as bait for fish. Mist hangs over the river, and eddies on the water's surface create beautiful patterns around rocks and reeds. Suddenly we hear a crack in the forest upriver. In the next moment, two tapirs swim by with their long snouts sniffing above the water's surface. The tapirs disappear around the river bend, and soon we will, too.

The natives, sitting at the boat's stern, look a little sly. We cannot guess what they are thinking and we don't know their language. Perhaps they consider us strange for taking so much trouble to travel deep inside the rain forest to see the animals.

But now what is this?

A large tree lies straight across the river. It probably fell during the last storm. We cannot get around it since the trunk rises about 8 inches (20 centimeters) above the water.

We unpack the heavy equipment from the boat and carry it along the tree onto land. This is a little nerve-racking. What if, we imagine, we drop the film and cameras into the water!

Now that the boat is lighter, we back up to gain speed and drive right over the tree. Although we almost fly over the trunk, the keel (bottom) of the boat is damaged, and it soon begins to leak. But the hole is not too large to repair, so we continue our journey up the river.

The swamp caiman is a reptile closely related to alligators (order Crocodilia). It is 5 feet (1.5 meters) long and lives mainly on fish. Crocodiles have not changed much in the last 65 million years. In rain forests there are many species. This caiman is among the smallest. The largest crocodile species live in Africa and grow as long as 24 feet (7.5 meters). Brazil

But stop!

Mattias's eyes react to the slightest movement in the forest, and he has just discovered a basilisk lizard.

A basilisk is an improbable animal that suddenly appears sitting amid riverbank vegetation and looking like something from the age of dinosaurs. But much smaller. A dino . . . sorry, a *basilisk* can grow to 3 feet (1 meter) long, including the tail.

Many of the over 38,000 species of lizard in the world live in rain forests. Some are more peculiar than others. Chameleons change color, and other lizards glide through the air from tree to tree. But basilisks can do what no other lizard can . . .

Yes, in a flash, our basilisk runs out onto the water to catch a dragonfly. According to the Bible, Jesus walked on water, so people have called the basilisk the Jesus Christ lizard. To avoid sinking and breaking the water's surface tension, this lizard must run for all it's worth. It looks really funky! But only younger specimens manage to run long stretches. Heavier basilisks soon sink below the surface after just a few steps and must resort to swimming. Most lizards are good swimmers. The basilisk, in addition, is a good diver that catches a fish or two when it feels like it. When the basilisk is on land, insects, scorpions, other lizards, and snakes must watch out. Even small birds and small mammals become basilisk food. Fruit and flowers also easily slip down into a basilisk's stomach.

Basilisk lizard. Brazil

Howler monkeys in South American and Central American rain forests search for fruit and leaves in the forest canopy. They may be seen on the ground sometimes. Brazil

The part of the Brazilian rain forest we are now traveling through is untouched by humans. High in a tree, a baby howler monkey wobbles along an unsteady branch. The mother howler monkey stays close behind to intervene should there be an accident. As rays of afternoon sun brighten them, Mattias takes photographs. In the next tree two macaws sit cozily.

We set up camp. Our guides build a simple hut. We put up our tent.

Before the sun sets, our guides fish in the river. We consider going for a swim. Then we notice that the natives have hauled up 4½ pounds (2 kilograms) of piranhas. We stop in our tracks. . . .

Piranha. Brazil

Piranhas are fish with a very bad reputation. Deciding what's true and what are merely fish stories may be hard. We know that piranhas feed primarily on other fish and carcasses. Some piranhas eat only plants. But we also know that piranhas have sharp teeth, and if they taste blood in the water, they may also attack larger naimals. We've been told that a single piranha with one bite can tear off a 1-cubic-inch (16-cubic-centimeter) chunk of flesh from its prey. And this may be fish lore. But we've learned that a whole school of hungry piranhas could attack a man and his horse, after they fall into the water, and in just a short time only their skeletons would remain. Perhaps. By the campfire we can all agree: smoked piranha are very tasty.

Centipede. Borneo

Night in the Rain Forest

Something scratches on the tent—right by my head! I fumble for the flashlight and shine it in the direction of the noise. A small animal is gnawing a hole through the tent wall. Then I see the silhouette of an 8-inch (20-centimeter) centipede running away over the tent.

Centipedes are predators. In the United States, Canada, and northern Europe, they don't grow more than a few inches or centimeters long and are harmless hunters of many small creeping things. In the rain forest centipedes can grow up to 12 inches (30 centimeters) long, and they're not content catching small bugs. Not even lizards, frogs, and mice are enough to satisfy a hungry centipede in the rain forest. It's not unusual to find a centipede visiting in the night. That's when most centipedes hunt. Even though they have a paralyzing poison in their jaws, it's only strong enough to give humans a painful bite, fever, and a few days or weeks of discomfort.

Tarantulas, called bird spiders, are the world's largest spiders. A tarantula can measure up to 10 inches (26 centimeters) from leg tip to leg tip. It would barely fit on this book page. Brazil

Night is a time when many peculiar creatures appear in the rain forest. It's also when many disappear . . .

We venture out on a night excursion. Something rattles a branch, we hear a few pitiful squeaks, and all is quiet once more. A bird spider has surprised a lizard in the dark.

Despite the name *bird spider*, birds are not a tarantula's most common source of food. Tarantulas usually catch spiders, insects, small frogs, and lizards. Do you feel sorry for the little lizard that became spider food? This is the way of nature and the "cruel" tarantula may soon be eaten itself. Perhaps even by a bird.

Geckos are fabulous lizards that have a fantastic ability to climb. Their large, flat feet are covered with millions of small grippers which enable them to climb upside down on the smoothest surface. Most of the 800 species of gecko hunt during the night. When you lie in a tent or house in the rain forest with a light on, it's fun to follow a gecko's adventures on the walls and ceiling. They hunt for insects. Large geckos hunt for small geckos. And we have seen them mate and in ecstasy lose their grip and fall down.

This gecko does not lick its mouth because it's hungry. It is trying to reach the water drops on its nose. Borneo

There's something likable about these small inhabitants of the rain forest. Geckos use tricks to escape enemies. Like many other lizards, they release the tail when attacked. The wiggling tail confuses the assailant and allows the lizard to escape. Asian house geckos can lose bits of skin, which bewilders an enemy. And flying geckos can unfold extra skin along the sides of the body, then glide away from danger.

The kinkajou is active at night. It's shy and we know little about its life. Brazil

Under the cover of darkness, a kinkajou pads away, hunting for something to eat. Perhaps it wants one of the many fruits of the rain forest, tasty leaves, or, why not, honey from a beehive. To reach the honey, the kinkajou uses its very long tongue.

Kinkajous live in South America and are very shy. They're almost entirely arboreal (tree-dwelling). You'll rarely find one on the ground. The kinkajou's tail wraps around branches, which is pretty handy if you like to climb trees to eat fruit. Holding on with its tail, a kinkajou can reach fruit hanging at the ends of long branches.

The part of the tail used for gripping is free from fur and almost functions as a hand. In South America especially, many animals have prehensile tails. Many monkeys, tree porcupines, and anteaters have them. In other parts of the world, other animals also have prehensile tails.

The pangolin (a.k.a. scaly anteater) has scales so tough that only humans, large cats, and hyenas can threaten a curled-up adult. Nigeria

Scaly anteaters look like pinecones and eat ants and termites. These animals are most peculiar. You may encounter a scaly anteater when walking at night in the rain forests of Africa and Asia. Like kinkajous, they have long tongues and a prehensile tail. But they are very different in appearance.

When a giant scaly anteater sends its long, sticky tongue into an anthill, ants stick to it like flies to flypaper. The tongue is up to 28 inches (70 centimeters) long. A giant scaly anteater can eat up to 200,000 ants a night.

In Africa, many scaly anteaters are killed for their tasty meat. In Asia, people make medicine from the scaly anteater's scales.

Poisonous animals often have bright colors, which make them easily recognizable.
Toads and other animals without *such a strong defense often have camouflage*
colors that protect them and make them hard to see. Brazil

At night in the rain forest, the smallest animals seem to make
the most noise. Katydids are insects with a fantastic ability to
make loud noises. Some species even sound like chainsaws saw-
ing wood and can be heard over ½ mile (1 kilometer) away. We
hear male katydids trying to attract females with their nightly
racket.

Even frogs want to participate in the rain forest choir with
their many different voices. Most of the world's 3,500 frog
species are found in rain forests, where constant humidity and
warmth make an easy life for a frog.

But even for the loudest members of the nighttime choir, it can be hard to make oneself heard in the rain forest. The dense foliage muffles all sounds. That's why it's important to work really hard to be noticed. And male frogs do just that. With croaking voices, they scare away other males and attract females. Listening to the peculiar choruses of frogs is interesting indeed.

Finding frogs to photograph can be tricky. Many have fantastic camouflage. The brightly colored frogs that are easier to spot defend themselves with poison glands, like the poison dart frog. Mattias must search with care.

The long legs and "fingers" of the banded tree frog make it an excellent climber. The frog's large eyes give it keen vision. They're good to have when small green insects on green leaves are the prey. Brazil

Fer-de-lance snake. Costa Rica

Snakes in the Forest

The fer-de-lance snake raises its head and looks directly into a giant eye. It's the camera lens the snake sees, with Mattias right behind, slowly creeping closer and closer. Mattias knows just how close he can crawl without risk, and he judges from the snake's behavior whether the snake is in a good mood.

It is important to know how animals behave if you want to study them or photograph them. Most animals flee people like us, who want to carefully observe them. Animals are so good at hiding, they are difficult to find.

When a snake feels the ground vibrate from our footsteps, it usually tries to slither away. Also, most snakes are so well camouflaged that it's hard to distinguish them from twigs and branches.

Most poisonous snakes are not interested in biting humans. They use their poison to kill small prey. Like other animals, snakes are smart enough to avoid wasting energy. When they feel trapped, some snakes will pretend to lunge with the mouth closed, just to scare you. That way, snakes waste no poison.

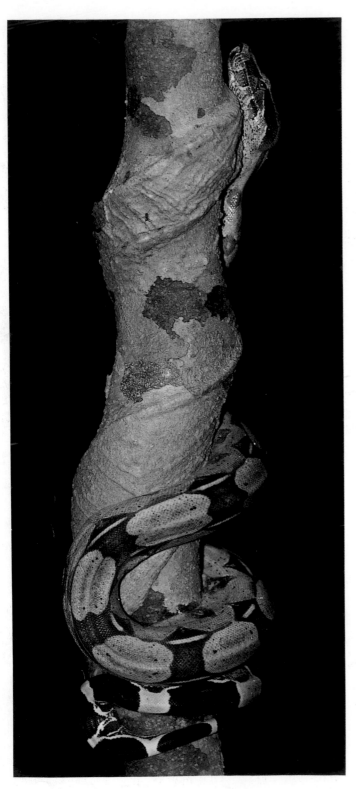

Only 10 percent of the snakes in the world are poisonous. And most of these snakes have a poison that's adapted to killing mice and frogs. Humans are *not* on any poisonous snake's regular menu. At most, we can only awaken a boa's or a python's appetite.*

Many tales relate how large snakes try to squeeze adventurers to death in the rain forest. But most of these stories are pure lies or fantasies. Just spotting a boa or python in the rain forest is feat enough. People who have been attacked by a snake have, in nearly all cases, tried to lift and play with it. It's no wonder the snake got a little upset.

Let's not focus on the danger of snakes. The idea of danger gets in the way of our amazement and admiration. Snakes are wondrously beautiful. Just look at how they move and their remarkable ways of adjusting the body to conform to any space.

Fer-de-lance snakes, boa constrictors, and a few other snakes have heat-sensitive pits on their faces. These are the

*However, if you live in Australia, you know that ten of the world's deadliest snakes live there. Few are nonpoisonous.

This red-tailed boa constrictor is middle size, and most grow no longer than 10 feet (3 meters). There are also small boas, and the anaconda, the largest, can grow to 36 feet (11 meters) long and weigh 1,100 pounds (500 kilograms). Brazil

The large-headed tree snake is as thin as a pencil and 3 feet (1 meter) long. At night it hunts for frogs and lizards. Brazil

most temperature-sensitive organs in the animal kingdom. With them, these snakes can sense temperature differences as little as .03° Fahrenheit (.001° Centigrade). In darkness they can create a heat image of their surroundings and find prey, usually small, warm mice or birds.

Some snakes can live without food for over two years. In the rain forest a female snake can have babies several times, years after she last mated. She saves the sperm from the last mating and draws it out when it's time to have baby snakes again.

A few snakes can even fly. The Asian paradise snake sucks in its stomach and expands its ribcage to transform itself into a glider. That's how this snake moves from tree to tree, hunting for frogs and lizards.

A green tree snake swallows a gecko. Borneo

Fight for Survival

One moment a gecko searches for beetles and lizard "candy." The next moment, the gecko finds itself disappearing down a snake's throat. No habitat on earth feels as much alive as the rain forest, but death may lurk behind any tree branch, blossom, or leaf.

In this constant battle for survival among various animals and plants, marvelous adaptations occur. An insect that looks like a leaf is hard for hungry birds to discover. That's why many insects have become more leaflike during the last several millennia. Others resemble twigs, which allows them to escape notice and avoid being eaten. Small poison dart frogs have developed a potent poison that keeps predators away. Many poisonous animals have developed very bright colors that function as warning signs and keep other animals from eating them by mistake.

The rain forest has been called both an enormous pantry and a large pharmacy. Trees and other plants with the tastiest fruit entice the most monkeys, birds, and other animals. These fruits find their way into the animal's stomach, and the seeds are usually spat out or excreted. That's how seeds may travel far from the original tree. And delicious plants can be spread more effectively than plants with less tasty fruit.

Leaves are very important for plants and help them grow well. That's why many plants have developed poisons to keep away leaf-eating animals. Sometimes these poisons, when used in very small quantities, act as useful medicines. Many everyday medicines have been derived from rain forest plants. Many more medicines may still be discovered, if we preserve the world's rain forests.

Rain forest. Brazil

High in the Trees

Rain forest trees reach 130 to 200 feet (40 to 60 meters) high. Over 50,000 different tree species are in rain forests around the world. About 1,000 species are in the United States and Canada. And in the smaller, northern country, Sweden, there are only 40 tree species.

Standing on the ground in the rain forest, you almost feel like a lobster on the ocean floor. The sun-drenched, green rain-forest canopy seems so beautiful, fascinating, and unreachable up there. If you want to peek at what is happening in the canopy, like Mattias, you can climb up a liana (woody vine) that grows next to a tree or use rock-climbing gear. Perhaps you could even build a hideout atop a tree.

Natives use poison from the skin of poison dart frogs. A tiny amount of poison on an arrowhead makes it an effective weapon. Just .001 milligrams can kill a human. Costa Rica

The blanket of leaves in the rain forest's canopy is so thick that most sunshine is prevented from reaching the ground. More than 99 percent of the light may "get stuck" in the rain forest's ceiling. That means that less than 1 percent reaches the rain forest's floor.

Toucans are known as seed spitters. After they have eaten a berry, they spit out the seed and help the plant spread to new places. Costa Rica

Up by the light, most fantastic flowers and fruits, as well as many interesting animals, are found.

Toucans are birds that live on fruit and other things in South American and Central American rain forests. The toucan's impressive beak can be used for many things. First and foremost, the beak helps the bird collect food, of course, but it also helps frighten away other birds. Toucans easily scare smaller birds from their nests and then eat their eggs and babies. Even when a toucan is itself under attack, it can scare away a predator with a flourish of its colorful beak. When toucans are in a playful mood, they sometimes toss fruit to each other with their beaks.

Parrots of all kinds climb high into the crown of trees searching for food. But they also seem to have a pleasant time together. Parrots are very social animals that often chat with each other. About 328 species can be found in rain forests around the world.

A parrot's beak has a mobile upper part and contains a powerful tongue. Peeling fruit without the aid of its feet is no problem for this Amazon parrot that lives in Central and South America. Costa Rica

Grasshopper. Brazil

Grasshopper with a Carrottop

Can a grasshopper have just any sort of appearance?

The "carrot" is a growth on the grasshopper's head. Presumably, it helps other grasshoppers of the same species know that they are friends. If you want to mate, it's silly to court a grasshopper from another species. The carrottop may also warn animals that eat grasshoppers to stay away. Bad-tasting grasshoppers often sport bright colors or have some feature that makes them stand out. Birds and other animals that eat grasshoppers quickly learn to recognize the ones that taste gross and leave them alone.

Insects, spiders, and other arthropods are found everywhere in the rain forest. Scientists have identified nearly 1 million insect species, but perhaps a million more have yet to be discovered. About half of the insect species living in the rain forest are beetles. And a single tree in the rain forest may have more species of ant than can be found in all of Sweden.

More than 80,000 different insect species are known to live on the North American continent.

Three-toed sloth. Sloths live in Central America and South America. Brazil

An Animal Not in a Hurry

The sloth has a very fitting name; few animals are as slow. A sloth usually manages to move about 6½ feet (2 meters) in an hour. But an active sloth can travel about 176 yards (162 meters) an hour.

It's rare to find a sloth anywhere but in the trees. Over time, the sloth's paws evolved into gripping claws that remind us of a telephone-pole repairman's crampons. On the ground, a sloth is completely defenseless. In water, it can manage and swims well, though slowly.

Sloths belong in trees. That's where they eat, mate, and raise their young. But it may be difficult to discover one. Its greenish fur and slow movements help it evade predators. A sloth may be mistaken as a knot underneath the branch it clings to.

The green color of the sloth's fur is really from algae that live on the animal. Every strand in the sloth's fur has a crevice which traps moisture, and algae thrive as though living in a mini-aquarium. Several hundred insects also live and breed in a sloth's fur as well.

Multiple plants live on a tree emerging high above the rain-forest canopy. Brazil

Plants on Plants

Large tree branches often fall to the ground because they become too heavy with the many plants that grow on them. Perhaps the worst offender is the bromeliad. In a single flower, a bromeliad growing on a tree can collect up to 25 gallons (100 liters) of water. In the water, frogs lay eggs, insect larvae swim, and crabs crawl—all 130 feet (40 meters) aboveground.

Many beautiful orchid species can root directly on a tree trunk.

If the tree is unfortunate, a bird will spit out a seed from a strangler fig in the tree's crown. Then the strangler fig will grow down around the tree from the crown and blanket the roots and leaves so that the tree eventually suffocates.

The insect-eating pitcher plant is nicer to the tree it grows on. It lures various insects into the fluid inside the pitcher plant, where they drown.

Lianas, large woody vines, also grow on other plants. Usually they begin growing high in a tree's branches and their winding vines can be several hundred yards (meters) long.

Plants that grow on other plants and that are not parasites are called epiphytes. These plants derive nutrients from air and water.

This orchid, which lives directly on the tree trunk, collects nutrients from rainwater that trickles down. Brazil

Monkey Business

Mattias is taking photos and I am watching a beautiful butterfly. Suddenly, she's standing there—a full-grown female orangutan with her curious baby.

We are close to a place where domesticated orangutans have been taught how to live in the wild. This orangutan, released perhaps a few years ago, seems both comfortable with humans and at home with nature.

Wild yet unafraid, the orangutan becomes curious about my bags. She waddles over to them and wants to take all my equipment with her into the forest. After a short tug-of-war, I succeed in rescuing my laptop computer but lose my camera. While the mother orangutan teaches her baby how to break a camera, we sneak away with the rest of our gear.

Orangutans spend most of their time in trees. Fruit makes up more than half of the apes' diet. In addition, they eat leaves, buds, insects, mineral-rich soil, bark, and sometimes bird eggs and small animals. Borneo

Even though orangutans are good at climbing trees, sometimes they fall and hurt themselves. Since female orangutans weigh 85 to 110 pounds (40 to 50 kilograms) and males 130 to 200 pounds (60 to 90 kilograms), not all tree branches and liana can support them. Borneo

A truly wild orangutan would never behave this way. We decide to venture further from civilization.

Despite our minor mishap, we remain charmed by orangutans. They have such a shrewd way of looking at us, and nothing could be more fun than watching a playful orangutan baby.

Orangutans live on the large Southeast Asian islands of Sumatra and Borneo. Decades ago, it was common to keep them as pets in huts; now that's prohibited. People who live in Borneo's rain forests have long believed that orangutans originated from a man who got into trouble with fellow villagers and fled into the forest. Even though humans are not *that* closely related to orangutans, we still share many traits. Orangutans are quite intelligent and have good memories. From year to year, they seem to remember where to find certain fruits and when these fruits will be ripe.

Orangutans feast at just the opportune moment on rain forest fruits, like durian, which tastes like a strawberry but smells like stinking fish. These apes also observe birds that eat the same fruits they favor. When these birds flock to a particular tree, orangutans hurry over to gather their share.

Monkey species differ in their climbing ability. Some monkeys climb much like humans, although with greater agility. Other monkeys jump from tree to tree, and the very skillful swing from branch to branch through the forest.

Gorillas, apes more than twice as heavy as orangutans, spend only 10 percent of their time in trees.

Chimpanzees, which are much smaller than gorillas, are better climbers. But they spend most of their time on the ground. Although orangutans can weigh as much as 220 pounds (100 kilograms), they move through the trees with ease. Smaller monkeys are more graceful, however.

Rain forests are nature's laboratories, where it conducts many experiments with amazing shapes and colors of plants and animals. This white uakari monkey, with bare face bright vermillion, is one of nature's beauties. Brazil

"Wow! What tasty fruit! If I hold one in my mouth and grab three in each hand, will that be enough?" We cannot know what a capuchin monkey is really thinking, but we do know it's really greedy. Brazil

Gibbons and spider monkeys seem capable of running straight through the forest canopy as though the law of gravity did not exist. Monkeys have adapted to different living conditions all over the world. The tiniest monkeys, the dwarf silk monkeys in South America, weigh one thousandth that of the largest gorilla. Most of the over 130 different monkey species in the world can be found in rain forests.

Apes, like gorillas, orangutans, and chimpanzees, are monkeys without tails or with just a short tail. Many can stand nearly erect, rather than walking on all fours.

Some monkey species have been mortal enemies. Sometimes chimpanzees hunt and eat other monkeys. But other groups of monkeys live together peacefully. Squirrel monkeys rely on capuchin monkeys, who are better at finding trees laden with fruit. That's why squirrel monkeys often tag along with capuchin monkeys.

Squirrel monkeys, found in South American rain forests, may be best known as Pippi Longstocking's pet monkey, Mister Nilsson. In the wild, outside story books, squirrel monkeys often live in groups and eat fruit, flowers, insects, and other nice little things, even small animals. If a bird attacks a group of squirrel monkeys, the monkeys simply let go of the branch and fall like ripe fruit from the tree. And they escape.

A squirrel monkey. Male squirrel monkeys do not fight, but they do frighten and threaten each other with outstretched legs and the usual display of maleness. Brazil

Gaton, a Borneo native.

People of the Rain Forest

His name is Gaton. Gaton is a Punan who lives in Borneo's rain forests. He was Mattias's quiet companion during his first rain forest expedition. No one since has been able to track animals and discover plants that Mattias has wanted to photograph as well as his old friend Gaton.

During our travels in the rain forest, we have met many people who live in the wild. And we have made many friends.

Deep in the rain forest you can meet native people who like rock music and zoom by motorboats to neighboring villages for parties. They continue to wear loincloths and to hunt with a blow dart and with a bow and arrow.

In one expedition, two natives set up camp nearby. We were astonished to see how easily they caught fish and lit a fire. They seemed to have complete mastery of life in the rain forest. Then, one day, one of the natives approached me as I was struggling to light the damp firewood and said, "It's much easier if you pour gasoline over it first."

But even to this day, some people in the deepest areas of the rain forest have never seen a car, never walked in a city, never heard of McDonald's, and don't know what television is. There aren't many, but they do exist. Perhaps they have seen an airplane pass high over the forest trees. Maybe they have heard noisy chainsaws and wondered about these rumbling machines invading the forest.

People living completely in the wilderness of the rain forest are quite knowledgeable about nature's many marvels. They have also learned how to live in the forest without harming it. We need to learn from them. We need to listen to their tales and to their thoughts.

Fire in the rain forest.

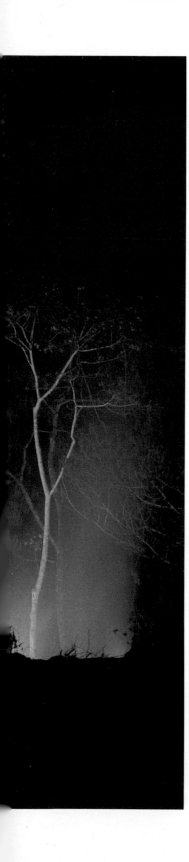

The Endangered Forest

A newborn baby sloth clings to its mother's fur. On a nearby branch, a green snake slithers away after an unsuccessful attempt to catch a frog. Baby parrots poke their heads out of the nest below, seeing for the first time a wonderful rain forest home that they will explore when their wings are strong enough. Hundreds of leaf-cutting ants carry one leaf each down from the tree's crown into their underground nest where mushrooms grow on the "transplanted" leaves. A butterfly warms its wings in the morning sun.

The worried sloth sniffs the air and its baby clings even tighter. The restless parrots fly back and forth beside their nest and nestlings. The snake is nearly shaken down from its branch by spider monkeys running in panic through the forest canopy, trying to escape.

The first wave of heat causes leaf-cutting ants to drop their leaves, the butterfly to fly away, and the baby parrots to curl up inside their nest.

The flames arrive suddenly, not giving the slow-moving sloth a chance. Mother and baby sloth burn to death along with the baby parrots, the snake, the ants, the flowers, this tree, the next tree, and the next . . . Soon, an entire rain forest has burned, and all those animals unable to escape have been burned to death.

In South America, people burn all or parts of rain forests to create temporary pastures and earn quick money.

In Asia, rain forests are cut down at an amazing speed to make single-use chopsticks and decorous wooden gift boxes for the Japanese. Other forests supply luxury boats and houses all over the world with exotic wood interiors.

Felling trees. Costa Rica

Lumberyard. Borneo

Why have rain forests been destroyed at such an amazing speed? The reasons are many. In a three-year period, rain forests the size of Sweden disappear. That's one football or soccer field every second! Animals and plants still undiscovered have become extinct.

In our travels in rain forests around the world—in Brazil, Costa Rica, Nigeria, and Borneo—we've witnessed this devastation. We've seen caravans of trucks and fleets of boats laden with lumber. If this pillaging continues, in thirty years no rain forests will remain.

That must not happen. We must save the fantastic world of the rain forest.

Save the Rain Forest!

These schooolchildren, on a trip to the rain forest, have a unique opportunity to observe and to learn. When they become adults, perhaps few rain forests may remain, unless *we* do something.

Many organizations around the world are working to preserve rain forests. Join one of them to help collect money to save these forests. Your friends may want to join, too. You could start study groups or perhaps even travel to the edges of rain forests to learn much about nature's careful ecology. If the governments of countries with rain forests recognize that the forests are more valuable when left intact than used as a source of lumber, perhaps they will also want to preserve them.

We do everything we can to spread this message in books and magazines, on the radio and on television, and in schools. Rain forests must be saved. Now it's your turn. And we all need to hurry!

Perhaps we will meet one day as we work to preserve rain forests worldwide. Let's hope we can still watch a sloth feed its baby, baby parrots try out their wings, and capuchin monkeys up to their usual monkey business high in the forests' trees.

Schoolchildren with their teacher on an excursion in Mount Kinabalu, a national park in Borneo. (above and left)

More About Rain Forests

You'll find **tropical rain forests** (the forests in this book) in lowland regions of the earth near the equator where temperatures are uniformly warm or hot and rainfall is abundant throughout the year. Tropical parts of Central America and South America, Africa, and Asia from India to the Philippines and northeastern Australia have tropical rain forests.

In some tropical mountainous regions, there are **tropical montane forests**. These are sometimes called **cloud forests**. (They're also called wet, mountain, temperate, and Andean forests.) Like tropical rain forests, they have high rainfall, but they have cooler temperatures and higher altitudes.

Not all rain forests are tropical. **Temperate rain forests** stretch in a narrow fog belt along North America's Pacific Coast from Alaska through British Columbia to northern California. More temperate rain forests are found in the southern Appalachian Mountains of the United States and in New Zealand. They receive over 100 inches of rain or snow a year.

What's called the rain forest **canopy** is the uppermost spreading branchy layer of the forest. **Emergents** are those few trees that grow higher than this canopy, sticking up above it. Below the canopy is the **understory**, which consists of the **middle layer**, **shrub layer**, and **herb layer**. The middle layer is just below the canopy, the shrub layer is just below that, and the herb layer is the closest to the ground. Animals and plants live in all layers of the forest from the tallest emergents down to the soil. They also live in rain forest rivers, swamps, and lakes.